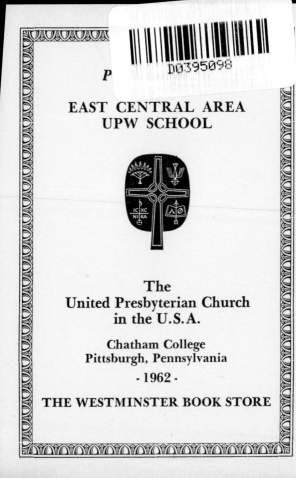

EAST CENTRAL AREA
UPW SCHOOL

The
United Presbyterian Church
in the U.S.A.

Chatham College
Pittsburgh, Pennsylvania

- 1962 -

THE WESTMINSTER BOOK STORE

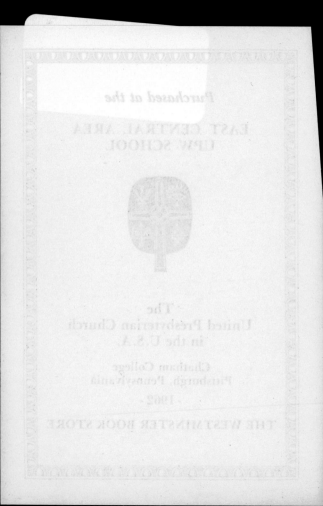

Family Prayers

Family
Prayers

Compiled by
MARJORY LOUISE BRACHER

Muhlenberg Press

Philadelphia   Pennsylvania

FOR

PETER AND ALICE

Library of Congress Catalog Card Number 62-8200
UB903   Printed in U.S.A.

PREFACE

An obstacle to daily prayer at the table or in family gatherings is the fact that we do not know what to say or how to say it. This collection of prayers is designed to overcome the monotony and impoverishment that plagues us all.

Prayer belongs to the life of the home. We need to give expression to our trust and joy in God. We need to hold up to him the duties and experiences of every day, not only in the privacy of individual prayer, but together, in words spoken aloud. This book is offered that we may be articulate in the very place where our first witness is to be made, within the family.

Spoken prayers in the home fill a place between personal prayer and public worship. They give essential witness to what is petitioned in private and confessed in church. It is in our everyday, here-and-now sharing of the life of each one in God, that this life acquires depth and reality.

MARJORY LOUISE BRACHER

Seattle, Washington

Our Father who art in heaven,
Hallowed be thy name.
Thy kingdom come,
Thy will be done,
On earth as it is in heaven.
Give us this day our daily bread;
And forgive us our debts,
As we also have forgiven our debtors;
And lead us not into temptation,
But deliver us from evil.
For thine is the kingdom and the power
and the glory, forever.

—Matthew 6:9-14

From the rising of the sun

THE CREATOR

O heavenly Father, who hast filled the world
with beauty, open our eyes to behold thy gracious hand in all thy works; that rejoicing in
thy whole creation, we may learn to serve thee
with gladness.

We praise thee, O God;
We acknowledge thee to be the Lord.
And we worship thy name ever,
World without end. Amen.

ADORATION

O praise the Lord with me,
and let us magnify his name together.
I will sing unto the Lord as long as I live,
I will sing praise to my God while I have
being.
O give thanks to the Lord for he is good;
For his steadfast love endures forever.

Lord Jesus,
All my blessings come from thee;
O how good thou art to me!

MORNING

Thanks be to thee, O blessed God,
For the night and its rest.
Thanks be to thee for this new day.
Shine upon us, O gracious Lord.

Most loving Father, let thy goodness and mercy so fill us with thankfulness, that both our words and our works this day, may tell forth thy praise.

Almighty God, our heavenly Father, who hast safely brought us to the beginning of this day: defend us in the same by thy mighty power; and grant that this day we fall into no sin, neither run into any kind of danger; but that all our doings being ordered by thy governance, may be righteous in thy sight; through Christ our Lord.

Holy, holy, holy, Lord God of hosts,
Heaven and earth are full of thy glory,
O Lord most high.

PRAISE

Praise the Lord,
Sing praise to our God.
For he is gracious;
His understanding is beyond measure.
He heals the brokenhearted,
And upholds those who are falling.
He is just in all his ways;
He is near to all who call.
He strengthens the bars of our gates;
And blesses our children.
The Lord is abundant in power;
He is faithful in all his words.
Praise the Lord,
Sing praise to our God.

PRAISE

Blessed be God for all that he is.
Blessed be God for all that he has done.
Blessed be God forever.

To Jesus, who has saved us, we give glory
and honor, worship and praise, now and forever.

Praise the Lord!
Praise him, sun and moon,
And all you shining stars.
Praise our Lord!

The day is thine

LITANY FOR TODAY

For the gift of another day:
We humbly thank thee.

By thy mercy grant us grace
    To live to thy praise;
    To meet our tasks gladly;
    To perform our duties faithfully:
        Hear us and help us.

Give us the grace
    Of speech and action;
    Of purity of heart;
    Of gentleness of temper and tongue;
    Of humbleness of spirit;
    Of contentment:
        Hear us and help us.

And in whatever comes,
    Whether joy or sorrow,
    Whether suffering or pleasure,
    Whether temptation or trial,
    Whether crisis or victory:
        Be present with us Lord,
        Keep us ever thine own.

SCHOOL

Let thy blessing, O Lord, be upon our work and study this day. Teach us to seek after truth, and enable us to attain it; but grant that as we increase in the knowledge of earthly things, we may grow in knowledge of thee, whom to know is life eternal.

O God, bless all who teach and all who learn. Grant that in humility we may ever look to thee, the source of all wisdom; through Christ our Lord.

WORK

Give us strength for our appointed duties,
that when we go to our work, we may take
 it up in good heart,
and when we cannot love our task, may yet
 be found faithful in it;
and all we do be well done, and fit for
 thine eyes to see.

Be thou with us every day,
In our work and in our play,
When we learn and when we pray;
 Hear us, Holy Jesus.

PROTECTION

Lord, have mercy upon us.
Protect and defend us:
    from the dangers of the road,
    from the hazards of our work,
    from the misuse of our powers.
Be gracious, and save us:
    from unemployment,
    from storm and flood,
    from war and desolation.
Spare us to them who lean upon us,
And in mercy grant us thy peace.

O God of mercy and love, keep all our dear ones in thy care. Strengthen our faith and trust in thee, that we be not anxious for the future, but look to thee in all our needs; through Christ our Lord.

FRUSTRATION

O Jesus, Son of Man:
When the everydayness of life
Deadens our spirits and pulls us low,
Speak, until we must hear!
Say to us again,
It is I who have chosen you.

ANXIETY

Almighty God and Savior, be our help now in this time of trouble. We need thy grace and thy strong hand. Keep us from despair and bitterness. Renew our hope and faith. Assure us of thy presence that we may have courage to face the trials of the days to come; through Christ our Lord.

O loving Father, preserve us from fear and anxiety. Do not let the clouds of this life hide us from the light of thine everlasting love, in Jesus Christ our Lord.

GUIDANCE

Direct us, O Lord, in all our doings with thy most gracious favor, and further us with thy continual help; that in all our works, begun, continued, and ended in thee, we may glorify thy holy name, and finally by thy mercy obtain everlasting life.

O God and Father of us all, sanctify this day by thy constant presence; in labor let us always work to thee, in leisure never grieve the Holy Spirit.

PATENCE

O Father in heaven grant us we pray thee, grace to bear with each other in all things. May we be ready to forgive, not once, but as we are forgiven by thee. Give us patience that we be not irritable nor resentful. Help us to believe the best of all men even as we would of ourselves. And do thou, O Lord, be long-suffering toward us, for the sake of Jesus Christ our Lord.

We beseech thee, O Lord, to keep our tongues from evil, and our lips from speaking guile; that, as thy holy angels ever sing thy praises in heaven, so with our tongues we may at all times glorify thee on earth.

UNREST

O Lord, our God,
Thou hast created us full of unrest;
Thou hast made us strangers in this world.
Make us restless in the meanness of our work.
Make us restless
In the greatness of thy commandment.
Make us restless

For the time that passes away
And every hour that is lost.
Make us restless that we are unholy
And unfitted to obey thee.

. . . .

We thank thee
That our work ends
And thy work begins.

PAY DAY

O God, all-knowing,
In humility we hold these fruits of our
   labor, mindful that in a world full of
   hunger, we have good food every day:
In thankfulness we take these gifts of thy
   providence, glad for work to do, and the
   ability to do it:
In turmoil of spirit we turn to thee before
   we buy clothes and groceries,
   anxious because of our many needs,
   torn by our desires.
Father, calm our discontent; control our
   longings. Give us wisdom to use what we
   hold, to our own best good, without harm
   to others, and in honor to thee;
   through Christ our Lord.

14

TEMPTATION

Lord Jesus Christ, strengthen us to resist the beginnings of evil before it take hold on us.

Make us to fear thee, and love thee; and follow thee by thy help, O Christ.

Lord Jesus Christ, tempted even as we: arm us, we pray, with a faith like thine, ready to answer the Tempter from God's own Word.

STRENGTH

O God, who knowest us to be set in the midst of so many and great dangers, and that by reason of the frailty of our nature we cannot always stand upright: Grant to us such strength and protection as may support us in all dangers, and carry us through all temptations; through Christ our Lord.

Father in heaven, we pray for one another, that though we be weak and our road be dark, we may in faith commit our way unto thee, who are able to hold us that we shall not fall.

MONEY

O Lord, give us a sincere faith that thou art ready and able to supply our need; and teach us to lay down our cares at thy feet, persuaded that while we trust in thy mercy we shall lack no good thing.

Give us open hands, O God, hands ready to share with all who are in want of the blessings with which thou hast enriched us. Deliver us from all meanness and miserliness. Let us hold our money in stewardship and all our wordly goods in trust for thee: to whom be now all honor and glory.

TRUST

Send the rains, thou Lord of rains.
Favor us, shower us with rain.
We remember Elijah in his prayers.
We too will pray.
We trust. We will see the rains.

God is our salvation.
We will trust and not be afraid.
The Lord God is our strength and our song.

UNCERTAINTY

Eternal God, who hast been the hope and joy of many generations, and who in all ages hast given man the power to seek thee and in seeking to find thee, grant us we pray thee, a clearer vision of thy truth, a greater faith in thy power, and a more confident assurance of thy love.

When the way seems dark before us, give us peace to walk trustingly:

When much is obscure to us, let us be all the more faithful in the little we can see clearly:

When the distant scene is clouded, let us rejoice that the next step is plain:

When what thou art is most hidden from our eyes, let us still hold fast to what thou dost command:

When insight falters, let obedience stand firm:

What we lack in faith let us repay in love.

FAITH

O God, who seest that we are prone to bring back the troubles of yesterday and to forecast the cares of tomorrow: give us grace to throw off our fears and anxieties, as our Lord commands, that this day we may live in faith, and be kept in thy peace.

O Lord, our God, give us such faith in thee, that we shall dare to go where thou art leading.

TROUBLE

O Lord, see our trouble!
Be near to comfort and help.
Hear our despairing cries;
Look on our sorrow.
Strength comes from thee:
Do not forsake us, O Lord.

O God, in whose love alone we learn the meaning of life, and in whose strength we bear its burdens, give us grace in everything to commit ourselves to thee, in faith that thou who hast brought us this far, art good to care for all thy children forever.

CONFIDENCE

Lord, we pray not for tranquility, nor that our tribulations may cease; we pray for thy spirit and thy love, that thou grant us strength and grace to overcome adversity.

> O Lord, let thy mercy be upon us,
> As our trust is in thee.

> Jesus, Friend of little children,
>   Be a friend to me;
> Take my hand and ever keep me
>   Close to thee.

REST

O Lord, support us all the day long of
    this troublous life,
until the shadows lengthen and the
    evening comes,
and the busy world is hushed,
and the fever of life is over,
and our work is done.
Then in thy mercy grant us safe lodging,
holy rest,
and peace at the last;
through Christ our Lord.

Bless our house

HOME

Father in heaven, we beseech thee to dwell
 where we dwell,
to be the light, joy, and peace of our home,
that our children may grow up in the man-
 hood of thy Son,
and that the memory of a godly and happy
 home, its prayers and its love,
may follow them with blessing,
when they go out to the work of the world.

  God bless the master of this house
   Likewise the mistress too,
  And all the little children
   That round the table go.

FAMILY

 O Lord, behold our family:
 We are thine.
 For our home, our food, our health,
 We thank thee.
 For making us dear to each other;
 For fun and work;
 For leading us day by day;
 We thank thee.
 Lord, keep us thine.

23

As the wild rose glorifies thee, O Lord, with its beauty and fragrance, so help us to glorify thee through our family.

MARRIAGE

Almighty God, by whose will we are united in marriage, grant us grace to live according to thy holy Word. Strengthen us in constant fidelity and true affection toward each other; sustain and defend us in all trials and temptations. Help us so to pass through this world in faith toward thee, and in communion with thy holy church, and in loving service one of the other, that we may enjoy forever thy holy benediction; through Jesus Christ our Lord.

Bless us, O Lord, that we may keep the promises we have made. Enable each to love, honor, and comfort the other. Be our stay in sickness and in health, and grant us long life together, in Christ our Lord.

GOD'S PRESENCE

Gracious God, be ever present with us, that thou mayest be known to be the defender of this household and the inhabitant of this dwelling.

Bless our home;
Make it a shelter from storm and night.
Let our windows be open to heaven,
And our doors for welcome.

May the love of God warm our hearts and the hearts of those who enter this house.

PARENTS

Father of all, we pray for those given to us in the close ties of family (*parents, brother, sister*): may they have the strength of a true faith, the joy of thy presence, and thy gracious care in all their needs; through Christ our Lord.

O God, our Father, we pray for our parents in thankful remembrance of their love to us: may thy heavenly light go always before them. In Jesus Christ our Savior.

MOVING

O God, our heavenly Father, gracious and
    unchanging:
We thank thee for all the joys we have known
    in this place;
For the beauty we have seen here;
For our friends and good neighbors.
We thank thee for thy presence with us, in
    good times and bad,
For the burdens turned into blessings.
Be with us in our new home, that all our wants
    may continue to be supplied;
And that we may both give and receive the
    blessings of true friendship;
In the name of Christ our Lord.

CHILDREN

O God, let the Word of Christ dwell in us
richly in all wisdom, that we may be able to
teach and admonish our children, with thankfulness in our hearts; and that whatever we do
in word or in deed, we may do everything in
the name of Jesus, giving thanks to thee, our
Father.

CHILDREN

Grant to our children healthy bodies and good
   minds.
Keep them from evil;
Arm them with thy truth;
Make them strong in the strength of Christ,
And let the beauty of the Lord our God be
   upon them.

Our Father, we thank thee for the joy of
having *this child* to love and to care for, and
to bring up in faith in thee. Grant us grace to
give *him* the full measure of our devotion, and
to set before *him* always a good example of the
Christian life. Bless us in our growth together,
and may our home be enriched by the simple
joys that come of loving and serving one another; through Jesus Christ our Lord.

O Lord, grant that our children may know
thee early and choose thee for themselves, that
in thy perfect freedom, they may enjoy thee,
both here in this life and forever.

BAPTISM

Most gracious and merciful Father, defend and keep (*child's name*) in thy grace, that *he* may never depart from thee but may always live according to thy will, and finally receive the fulness of thy promised kingdom; through Jesus Christ our Lord.

O loving and merciful God, grant that as we now glory in the beginnings of thy grace, we may also look forward to its completion.

Almighty God, let not the flame of faith, once kindled in our hearts, be quenched; but do thou continually feed and renew it.

CONFIRMATION

Almighty and merciful God, continue we pray, the work which thou hast begun: that (*name*), and we, may
Live in joyful obedience to thy Word,
Know thee more perfectly,
Love thee more fervently, and
Serve thee in every good work and deed, to the glory of thy name; through Jesus Christ our Lord.

O God, our Father, we thank thee for bringing us to a day of renewal and confirmation. Bless *thy servant* with such a measure of the Holy Spirit that *he* may grow in grace until life's end.

BIRTHDAYS

O God of surpassing goodness,
Who hast rounded our life with mystery,
Yet made us to be thine own:
We thank thee for all the days of our years,
And pray that both time and circumstance
May serve only to bring us closer to thee,
And all of life be to thy glory.

God in heaven who made you,
Look in love upon you.

O God, whose will is the end for which we were made, grant that we may live as branches of the true Vine, and so bear fruit to thee.

O Lord, our shepherd through all the years, let thy goodness and mercy follow us to the end, that we may be with thee forever.

THE ABSENT

Heavenly Father, we pray for our loved ones
who are in difficult places.
Defend them day by day with thy heavenly
grace;
Strengthen them in their trials and temptations;
Give them courage to face the perils that sur-
round them;
And help them to know the safety of those
who put their trust in thee; through Christ
our Lord.

Watch over our dear ones who are far away.
Bless to them the memories of home and child-
hood, and of us who pray for them. Lift upon
them the light of thy face. And though we are
absent one from another, keep us inseparable
in the love of Christ.

ILLNESS

O God our Father, hold us all in thy keeping. Be with us in the hours of sickness and pain. Give back to *our dear one* health and strength.

May we have sympathy with all who suffer.

And for every gift of healing and renewal, send us forth with thankful hearts to greater consecration; through Jesus our Lord.

SUFFERING

O Lord, who dost feel the pain of the world: look with mercy we beseech thee, upon *those* who in sickness and suffering are beyond the reach of human skill. To thee alone belongs the power of life, and these souls are thine. Of thy great love give *them* grace to endure bravely, and such an assurance of thy presence, that *they* may know peace.

O God, amid all uncertainties, deepen our faith, and make us ready to trust thee where we cannot see.

DEATH

Grant, O Lord, unto us and all who are bereaved, the faith and courage that come only of thee, to meet each day with steadfastness and patience; not sorrowing as those without hope, but in thankful remembrance of thy great goodness in past years, and in the sure expectation of a joyful reunion with those we love. This we ask in the name of Jesus our Savior.

SORROW

Heavenly Father, to whom all sorrows are known, grant us the comfort of thy grace in our loss and loneliness. We thank thee for the love that has been ours and even now remains. Give us each day strength to bear our burden, and keep us in thy care until life's end; through Christ our Lord.

Almighty, eternal God, still let the blessed promise be fulfilled; leave us not comfortless; abide with us forever; through Christ our Savior.

REMEMBRANCE

Eternal Father, we give thee thanks for all thy servants who have lived and died in the faith of Jesus, and especially for those who were the joy of our hearts and who worshipped with us in thy holy house. We give thee thanks for the happiness that is theirs, freed from the bonds of earthly life, and for the sure promise of Christ, that they and we, redeemed from all evils, shall walk hereafter together and with thee, in love and light eternal.

O eternal God, we bless and praise thee for those most dear to our remembrance who have gone before us to their rest in thee.

Let us praise God for our fathers, and their
fathers before them: those
Who lived in the faith, and taught it to their
children;
Who served God in fear and trust;
Who in sorrow, pain, joy, or defeat,
Through wars, famine, peace, or plenty,
Ran their course in hope
For the glory set before them.

For this great company of men and women,
Those we remember and those we never knew,
We give thee thanks, our God.
Enable us, as thou enabled them, to know the
life that is true life,
To conquer through him who loves us, and
To be faithful unto death; through Christ our
Lord.

HOPE

O Father, when our spirits shrink before the mystery of life and death, let us thy children be persuaded that nothing can separate us from thy love, but that whether we live or die, we are safe in thy keeping.

Grant that when our last hour comes, we be not troubled nor dismayed, but commending our spirits into thy merciful hands, O Father, and firmly trusting in the merits of our Savior, we may obtain a peaceful death and a happy entrance into glory.

And our neighbor

DIVINE CARE

O God, the Father of all mankind,
We commend to thy holy keeping:
> All who tonight are far from home and
>   friends;
> All who tonight must lie down hungry and
>   cold;
> All who suffer pain;
> All who are kept awake by anxiety or sus-
>   pense;
> All who are facing danger;
> All who must toil or keep watch while others
>   sleep;

Give to them all, we pray, such a sense of thy
presence with them as may turn their loneliness into comfort and their trouble into peace.

DELIVERANCE

This is our poverty:
That we do not belong to each other
Nor serve one another.
We go each his own way
And do not care for our neighbor.
We pray thee, O Lord:
Redeem us from this estrangement,

37

Redeem us out of this loneliness.
Deliver us from the sin that divides us.
Join us closely in true love.
Have mercy upon all thy children.
Lord, we would love:
Take away our un-loving.

THE HOMELESS

Look with pity, O Lord, upon the broken families of the earth, driven from their homes to wander as refugees in strange places.

Look with pity on this whole generation of thy children, so far strayed from thy ways.

Look with pity upon us all, and have mercy, O Lord.

Increase, O God, the spirit of neighborliness among us, that in peril we may uphold one another, in suffering tend one another, and in homelessness or loneliness befriend one another.

PEACE

O God, who hast led man by thy Spirit to forsake the jungle and its cruelties for the city and its laws, lead us to the vision of a world without war and of mankind at peace. As we are bound together by commerce and science, so may our hearts be united in love. Help us to live in the unity of thy family, without distinction of class or color, O Creator, and Father of us all.

Let thy power, O Christ, be in us all, to share the world's suffering and redress its wrongs.

IN WAR

Grant, O God of compassion, that with malice toward none, with charity to all, with firmness in the right as thou givest us to see the right, we may strive to bind up the nation's wounds, and to do all which may achieve and cherish a just and lasting peace among ourselves and all nations.

GOVERNMENT

O God, who of old time didst raise up rulers and lawgivers for thy people, guide us to a right choice of men to serve in the governing of this (*land, city, town, etc.*). And to those who shall be chosen, give right judgment and a brave and upright heart; that fearing none and seeking no man's favor, they may give true votes. Keep their deliberations free from bias and bitterness; make their decisions honest, just, and wise; so that in this (*land*) we love, righteousness may flourish.

Cast down, O Lord, all the forces of cruelty and wrong. Defeat all selfish and worldly-minded schemes, and prosper all that is conceived among us in the spirit of Christ and carried out to the honor of his name.

FOR ALL MARRIAGES

O God, who created us man and woman,
And made us to live in families,
We ask thy blessing on all marriages,
Among us, our neighbors, and all people:
Bind husband and wife together
In the love which creates and fulfills,
In love which knows its source in thee.
Give the will to fidelity;
Give the will to honor;
Give love that *is not possessive*
Nor *touchy. Give love that knows*
No limit to its endurance,
No end to its trust.

We have beheld His glory

ADVENT

Our God, we have waited for thee:
Come to us, and save us.
Stir up thy power, and rescue us from sin,
That we may serve thee.
Come, to be light to our darkness;
Come, to bring life for our death.
Stir up our hearts, to make ready thy way.
O Lord, we wait:
Come!

CHRISTMAS

God bless our house this holy night,
    And all within it.
God bless the candles that we light.

    O Holy Child of Bethlehem,
    Descend to us we pray;
    Cast out our sin, and enter in,
    Be born in us today.

Grant us, dear Lord, a place beside
The Baby Christ at Christmastide.

CHRISTMAS

O ye heights of heaven, adore him;
    Angel hosts his praises sing;
Powers, dominions, bow before him,
    And extol our God and King.

The Christmas candles are burned out;
    the carols have died away;
      the star is set;
      all the radiant song-filled night is past.
Thou alone, the eternal, remainest,
    and thou art enough:
Christ, our Lord!

LENT

Lord Jesus, we humbly pray:
That we may never be separated from thee;
That we may never stray away from thee;
That we may never be drawn away from thee;
That we may never carry any mark but thine,
    —the seal of thy cross;
That all men may know we are thy disciples.

Jesus, of thee shall be my song,
To thee my heart and soul belong;

All that I have or am is thine,
And thou, blest Savior, thou art mine,
 Jesus, my Lord, I thee adore!
 O make me love thee more and more.

EASTER

We remember the manger.
We remember the cross.
We remember the empty tomb.
We remember the precious words:
 God so loved!
O Lord Jesus Christ,
Receive our adoration and praise
This happy day;
Accept our thankful love.

O Lord, who has set before us the great
hope that thy kingdom shall come on earth as
it is in heaven: We rejoice in each manifesta-
tion of thy power, and thank thee for each
promise fulfilled, in Jesus Christ, our Savior.

A lamp to our feet

THE ETERNAL WORD

O God, whose restoring love has been at work from the beginning, and whose promises are until the end: we thank thee for the witness of the Bible, for the living presence of the Holy Spirit, and for all the evidences of thy great goodness to us thy children, in Christ our Lord.

BIBLE READING

O Christ, we come into thy presence, and how beautiful it is! There is no place so beautiful as the place where thou art.

Bless our hunger and thirst as thou hast promised, that we may come to know thee truly, and to love thee for what thou art.

Grant, O Lord, that we may receive thy Word with meekness and feel its power, and so be transformed into the likeness of Christ our Savior.

BIBLE READING

O Word of God incarnate,
    O Wisdom from on high,
O Truth unchanged, unchanging,
    O Light of our dark sky;
We praise thee for the radiance
    That from the hallowed page,
A lantern to our footsteps,
    Shines on from age to age.

O God, sow in our hearts the precious seed of thy truth; then grant it to grow through prayer and obedience, to the fruit of eternal life; through Christ our Lord.

COMFORT

Defend us, O Lord, from any doubt of thy gospel, and keep our thoughts when our faith is assailed, so that even in the dark night of the soul, we may fear no evil, because thou art with us, and the rod and staff of thy Word shall guard, comfort, and strengthen us.

Restore to us the joy

PENITENCE

O God, we confess that we have sinned against thee, in thought, word, and deed. Have mercy upon us, Lord, after thy great goodness. Take away our offences and cleanse us from our sins.

O Lord, cast out of us every evil thought and desire; all envy, anger, and remembrance of wrongs done to us. Take away every act and thought that is contrary to thy will.

Almighty God, make us to love that which thou dost command.

PENITENCE

Save us, O Lord, from pride and self, from setting a bad example, from leading others into temptation, and causing our brother to stumble.

From these and all the evils we have feared and prayed against, save us, through Christ our Lord.

Jesus, Savior, wash away
All that has been wrong today;
Help me every day to be
Good and loving, more like thee.

MERCY

Father, merciful and compassionate: with humble hearts we receive thy forgiveness, in the name of Jesus Christ our Savior.

Almighty God, our heavenly Father, who in mercy gave thy Son to die for us: we thank thee for the forgiveness of our sins, and for the power to become thy children, and for the gift of the Holy Spirit.

GRACE

Almighty God, unto whom all hearts are open, all desires known, and from whom no secrets are hid: cleanse the thoughts of our hearts by the inspiration of thy Holy Spirit, that we may perfectly love thee, and worthily magnify thy holy name; through Christ our Lord.

O thou in whose boundless being are laid up all treasures of wisdom and truth and holiness, grant that through constant fellowship with thee, the true graces of Christian character may more and more take shape within us; through Christ our Lord.

FORGIVENESS

Pour down upon us the abundance of thy mercy, forgiving us those things whereof our conscience is afraid, and giving us those good things we are not worthy to ask, but through the merits of Jesus our Lord.

Father, have mercy upon us; forgive us all that is past, and grant that we may hereafter serve and please thee in newness of life, to the glory of thy holy name.

DEVOTION

O most merciful Redeemer, Friend, and Brother,
May we know thee more clearly,
Love thee more dearly,
And follow thee more nearly,
For thine own sake.

O Lord God, grant us always, whatever the world may say, to content ourselves with what thou wilt say, and to care only for thine approval, which will outweigh all worlds; for Jesus Christ's sake.

SERVING GOD

Teach us, good Lord, to serve thee as thou
    deservest:
  To give and not to count the cost;
  To fight and not to heed the wounds;
  To strive and not to seek for rest;
  To labor and not to ask for reward,
Saving the knowledge that we do thy will.

O God, forasmuch as without thee we are
not able to please thee: mercifully grant that
thy Holy Spirit may in all things direct and
rule our hearts.

LOVE

We acknowledge, O God, that love is the
great want of our hearts. Enable us by thy
grace to live in true love for thee and for one
another, that we may keep thy commandments
and so dwell with thee now, and forever.

As the warm spring breezes melt the ice and
provide living water for the fields, may the
warm love of God melt and refresh our hard
hearts.

JOY

O God, who made us in thine image,
    Sought us when we turned away,
    Loved us, the unlovely,
    And bought us back:
We thank thee for the miracle of thy love,
    In Jesus the Good Shepherd,
    In Jesus of the Welcoming-heart,
    In Jesus of the Healing-touch,
    In Jesus the Light,
    In Jesus our Lord.
Thee we adore, eternal God,
    God of our great joy.

CONSECRATION

O Lord, may thy will be our peace,
    thy love our rest,
    thy service our joy,
    thy promises our hope.

JUDGMENT

Disquiet us over our sin,
Over the sin of the whole world.
Make our disquiet such
That we may be prepared at all times
For thy judgment.
Yet though our hearts be never so unquiet,
Let us hold fast in faith.
Let us go forward
In the longing for the dawn
Of thy kingdom.

Almighty God, whose loving hand has given
us all that we possess; grant us grace that we
may honor thee with our substance, and re-
membering the account we must one day give,
may be faithful stewards of thy bounty;
through Jesus Christ our Lord.

Let us kneel before the Lord

SUNDAY

O God of peace who has taught us that in
   returning and rest we shall be saved,
in quiet and confidence shall be our strength;
by the might of thy spirit lift us, we pray thee,
   to thy presence,
where we may be still and know that thou art
   God;
through Jesus Christ our Lord.

O Lord, accept us, as with humble and
grateful hearts we go now to worship thee; and
grant that the prayers and the gifts we offer
this day may be pleasing in thy sight.

THE CHURCH

O Jesus, Master and Lord: guard our church
   from human plans and purposes;
   from coldness;
   from the paralysis of formalism;
   from the devices of the devil;
Fill our church with thy spirit.
Keep her living,
      loving,
      testifying;
      seeking,

rescuing,
restoring;
guarding,
holding,
adoring;
looking for thy return.

WORSHIP

Bless all who worship thee, from the rising of
the sun to the going down of the same:
> Of thy goodness give us,
> With thy love inspire us,
> By thy spirit guide us,
> By thy power protect us;
In thy mercy receive us now and always.

As we enter into thy holy house,
Be thou with us, O Lord;
As we return to common duties,
Go thou with us.
In worship and in work alike,
Be thou with us,
'Til work itself be worship,
And our every thought be thy praise.

COMMUNION

O Lord, in love and mercy, prepare us to receive thyself. Empty our minds of every thought, desire, hope, or fear which may keep thee away.

O Father, we give thee thanks for the blessed sacrament in which we remember our Lord's death and taste his living presence.

We give thee thanks for the pardon of our sins and for the power to lead a new life.

We give thee thanks for the hope and confidence brought to us in Jesus Christ.

AFTER WORSHIP

Confirm thy Word, O Lord, by the testimony of the Holy Spirit within us; and bless us who have worshipped,
    with a more steadfast will,
    a more loving spirit,
    prepared in everything to honor thy laws,
    and to serve one another.
Let thy good power act and operate within us,
    through Christ our Lord.

WORLD MISSION

We pray, O Lord, for those who labor for thee, in distant places and near. Sustain their strength and their faith, that they may willingly sow, water, or reap, as thou hast appointed them, seeking not the praise of men, but ever glorifying thee.

O Lord, speed the day when all the earth may stand with open doors and open hearts, awaiting the coming of thy Son.

PASTOR

We thank thee for giving us a pastor.
Make him strong and wise
    to declare thy gospel,
    to point out thy way,
    to condemn our sin,
    to rebuke unrighteousness,
    to show thy restoring love.
Give him grace to live what he teaches,
Let him in all things be faithful.
Then do thou give to us the hearing ear, the understanding heart, and the devoted will; through Jesus Christ our Lord.

*Thy loving kindness
is better than life*

PROVIDENCE

Father in heaven, by whose providence we have come to the end of the year, we turn to thee with gratitude for the past, and in trust for the future. Whatever changes come, grant that we may love thee with a constant love, and loving thee, do thy will; through Christ our Lord.

DAILY BREAD

O Lord, thou hast given us all that we need and more. May we thank thee humbly and serve thee willingly.

> God bless our meat,
> God guide our ways,
> God give us grace,
> Our Lord to please.

Blessed be the Lord God for all his mercies to us, in Christ Jesus.

DAILY BREAD

O thou who clothest the lilies
And feedest the birds of the sky,
And leadest the lambs to pasture
And the hart to the waterside,
Who hast multiplied loaves and fishes
And converted water into wine,
Do thou come to our table
As guest and giver to dine.

We give thanks unto thee, O God, for thyself, and all these things besides.

Lord, gratitude we offer all
    Who labor that we may be fed;
O dignify our toil for them,
    Bring kinship through our daily bread.

Noontime is here, the board is spread.
Thanks be to God who gives us bread.

Thank you for the world so sweet;
Thank you for the food we eat;
Thank you for the birds that sing;
Thank you, God, for everything!

BLESSING

Brother and Lord, among thy people sitting,
      Lord of our toil,
      Bestower of our rest,
Lord of our feast, to thee as is most fitting,
      Praises and thanks we bring,
      Our whole heart's best:
      Jesus, be thou our guest.

Bless the Lord, O my soul:
And all that is within me, bless his holy name.
Bless the Lord, O my soul,
And forget not all his benefits.

BLESSING

O God who has given us gifts such as our
fathers neither knew nor dreamed of: grant
that we forget not the things which are of the
spirit, lest having gained the whole world, we
lose our own soul.

Bless these gifts, O God,
From whom all goodness springs;
Make clean our hearts and feed our souls
With good and joyful things.

GRATITUDE

The earth has yielded its increase:
  God, our God, has blessed us.

We give thanks now for the grace that
comes through our Lord Jesus Christ, the love
that is of God the Father, and the fellowship
that is ours through the Holy Spirit.

O God, our Creator and Father in heaven,
We thank thee for the pleasures of this day:
For the joy of being alive,
For work to do and strength to do it,
For fun and play,
For rest when tired.
Grant that in all days, good or bad,
We may desire and know thy watchful pres-
  ence.

Even the night shall be light

EVENING

Day is done;
We give thee thanks, O Lord.
The night falls;
We give thee praise.
We have been delivered from evil;
We have been kept in safety.
Praise be to thee, O God.

> Jesus, I kneel down to say
> Thank you for another day.

The Lord bless us and keep us. The Lord make his face shine upon us and be gracious unto us. The Lord lift up his countenance upon us and give us peace.

SLEEP

O Lord, our God, when we are wearied with the day's work, refresh us with quiet sleep, that being strengthened with the help which our weakness needs, we may be devoted to thee both in body and mind.

God the Father bless us,
God the Son defend us,
God the Holy Spirit keep us,
Now and forever. Amen.

I will lay me down in peace, and sleep. For thou, Lord, only, makest me dwell in safety.

NIGHT

Father in heaven,
As this day closes
We turn again to thee,
Our soul's delight.
We thank thee for thyself,
Most of all for thyself.
We wait for the morning
When all thy promises shall be fulfilled.
We look to the morning:
Amen. Come, Lord Jesus.

Save us, O God, waking; guard us sleeping;
that awake we may watch with Christ, and
asleep we may rest in peace.

SAFETY

Jesus, tender shepherd hear me,
    Bless thy little lamb tonight;
Through the darkness be thou near me,
    Keep me safe till morning light.

      Good night! Good night!
      Far flies the light;
      But still God's love
      Shall flame above,
      Making all bright.
      Good night! Good night!

O Lord our God, as we began the day with praise of thee, so do we end it. Refresh us and our loved ones with sleep. Bring us to the morning in health and hope; then direct our ways and our work to thy glory; through Christ our Lord.

SOURCES OF THE PRAYERS

Page

13.　M. L. Bracher.
　　　Roman Breviary.
　　　Selected from Daniel J. Fleming, in "The Church
　　　　　in Germany in Prayer," from *The World At
　　　　　One in Prayer* (New York: Harper & Brothers,
　　　　　1942).
14.　M. L. Bracher.
15.　Composite.
　　　M. L. Bracher.
　　　Book of Common Prayer.
　　　Author unknown.
16.　St. Ignatius Loyola.
　　　Adapted from John Baillie, *op. cit.*
　　　from *The World At One in Prayer.*
　　　Isaiah 12:2.
17.　John Baillie, *op. cit.*
18.　Adapted and selected from James Ferguson, *op. cit.*
　　　Ibid.
　　　M. L. Bracher.
　　　Selected from James Ferguson, *op. cit.*
19.　Savonarola.
　　　Evening Suffrages, *Service Book and Hymnal*
　　　Walter J. Mathams.
　　　Sarum Breviary.
23.　James Ferguson, *op. cit.*
　　　Traditional English.
　　　M. L. Bracher.
24.　Adapted from the Korean, in *The World At One
　　　　　in Prayer.*
　　　Adapted from the Order for Marriage, *Service
　　　　　Book & Hymnal.*
　　　Ibid.
25.　*Gelasian Sacramentary.*
　　　Adapted from James Ferguson, *op. cit.*
　　　M. L. Bracher.
　　　Ibid.
　　　Ibid.
26.　*Ibid.*
　　　From Colossians 3:16-17, Revised Standard
　　　　　Version.

Page

27. James Ferguson, *op. cit.*
    Adapted from Stuart R. Oglesby, *op. cit.*
    Adapted from James Ferguson, *op. cit.*
28. Adapted from the Order for Baptism of Infants,
    Service Book & Hymnal.
    Adapted from the *Leonine Sacramentary.*
    Presbyterian Forms of Service.
    Arranged from the Order for Confirmation, *Service
    Book & Hymnal.*
29. Composite.
    M. L. Bracher.
    Ibid.
    Ibid.
    Ibid.
30. Adapted from Stuart R. Oglesby, *op. cit.*
    James Ferguson, *op. cit.*
31. Adapted from *Prayers for All Occasions.* Forward
    Movement.
    Ibid.
    Selected from James Ferguson, *op. cit.*
32. Source unknown.
    Adapted from *Prayers for All Occasions.* Forward
    Movement.
    Book of Common Prayer.
33. James Ferguson, *op. cit.*
    Ibid.
    M. L. Bracher.
34. *Ibid.*
    Book of Common Worship.
37. John Baillie, *op. cit.*
    Selected from "The Church in Germany in
    Prayer," *op. cit.*
38. Selected from a Chinese prayer, in *The World
    At One in Prayer.*
    Adapted from "Our Shelter Prayer."
39. Adapted from the prayer copyrighted by Canon
    J. B. Goodliffe.
    John Baillie, *op. cit.*
    Adapted from Abraham Lincoln.

Page

40. Lionel James, in *Jubilate Deo*. (New York: Oxford University Press, Inc.
    John Baillie, *op. cit.*
41. M. L. Bracher. (J. B. Phillips' tr. of Corinthians 13, from *The New Testament in Modern English* (New York: The Macmillan Company, 1958).
45. M. L. Bracher.
    Selected lines by Eleanor Farjeon, from "This Holy Night," in *Poems for Children* (Philadelphia: Lippincott, 1951).
    Phillips Brooks.
    Willis Boyd Allen, in "Christmastide."
46. From an early Christian hymn.
    Author unknown.
    Selected from Paul Zeller Strodach, *op. cit.*
    Henry Collins (1827-1919).
47. M. L. Bracher.
    Ibid.
51. *Ibid.*
    Prayer from India, in *The World At One in Prayer*.
    Source unknown.
    Adapted from Ancient Scottish prayers.
52. William Walsham How (1823-97).
    M. L. Bracher.
    James Ferguson, *op. cit.*
55. Adapted from *Prayers for All Occasions*. Forward Movement.
    Adapted from the Liturgy of St. James.
    From the Collect for the 14th Sunday after Trinity, *Book of Common Prayer*.
56. Adapted from James Ferguson, *op. cit.*
    Frances Ridley Havergal (1836-79).
57. M. L. Bracher.
    Ibid.
    Ancient Collect.
    John Baillie, *op. cit.*
58. *Book of Common Prayer*.
    Ibid.

85

Page
74. James Ferguson, *op. cit.*
    Arranged from Phillips' tr. II Corinthians 13:14, *op. cit.*
    M. L. Bracher.
77. *Ibid.*
    Lysbeth Boyd Borie, in "Just for Jesus," in *Poems for Peter* (Philadelphia: Lippincott, 1928).
    Numbers 6:24-26.
78. *Leonine Sacramentary,* altered.
    Traditional blessing.
    Psalm 4:8.
79. M. L. Bracher.
    Roman Breviary.
80. Mary Lundie Duncan (1814-40).
    Attributed to Victor Hugo.
    Adapted from James Ferguson, *op. cit.*

INDEX

Subjects and Occasions

86

88

PRAYERS FOR YOUNG CHILDREN

Type used in this book
Body, 11 on 12, Fairfield
Display, Futura
Paper: "R" Standard White Antique